T0129844

MOMS *in* MAYHEM

Lindsey Winkler

authorHOUSE®

AuthorHouse™
1663 Liberty Drive
Bloomington, IN 47403
www.authorhouse.com
Phone: 1 (800) 839-8640

Published by AuthorHouse 03/27/2019

ISBN: 978-1-5462-7522-0 (sc)
ISBN: 978-1-5462-7521-3 (e)

Library of Congress Control Number: 2019900240

Print information available on the last page.

This book is Dedicated to my Son:
Thank you for bringing Peace to my Chaos
And teaching me how to be a parent.

INTRODUCTION

What is the difference between a Mom who is in total chaos and the Mom who has it all together?

Mind Set.

This book is a how-to guide into creating the time and the perfect mindset to take on life as a mother, one moment at a time. Learn to be able to handle everyday curveballs thrown at you, manage your time and create space in your life to alleviate stress during hard moments in the day. We, as parents, are teaching life skills to our children, developing children who are wholesome contributions towards society. Preparing them to take on life with responsibility, confidence, respect, and honor.

This book will give you the skills to quiet the yelling and the chaos from your everyday life. Being a Mother, teacher, and nanny for many years has taught me how to get on the child's level and know what they need when their reaction is beyond acceptable. Staying calm and collected during crazy times is just one of many skills I have honed over the years and I am now sharing my secrets with you. Remember the skills taught in this book need to be used on a regular basis. Consistency is what makes the tools work. We are creatures of habit and developing good habits is not easy but with diligence is well worth it. Enjoy and I hope this book changes your life. I know that while raising kids I have had good days and bad days but at the end of the day it is all about how you feel. Let's turn the bad days into bad moments and conquer each day one breath at a time.

CHAPTER 1

Control the Chaos

Your world is spinning your being pulled in 5 different directions. The phone is ringing, children are screaming, dog barking, and demands are being thrown your way at 100MPH. Chaos, pure and genuine chaos is a Mother's daily. You are expected to do everything, know everything, where it is/goes and accomplish it all in seconds. "Honey, where is my jacket? Mom, where are my shoes? Did you pack my lunch? Did you wash my lucky socks for my game tonight? Did you iron my shirt I have that big meeting today?" all this before 7am.

Welcome to Motherhood. If this sounds familiar say "I."

Some people have it all together and others have chaos.

The question is how do we control the chaos in the busy world in which we live and how do we do it without losing our minds? The answer is one moment at a time. One step in the right direction a few small things added to your daily routine to help smooth out all the wrinkles. The chaos will always be a part of your day, but it is up to us to take the time to manage the chaos or let it manage us.

It is up to us to live in the eye of the storm.

These next few chapters will give you the tools needed to manage the chaos and prepare yourself to handle the world around you on a day to day basis.

Creating Space:

Have you ever been stuck in a traffic jam? Of course you have, the person in front of you just got cut off by the person next to him which caused him to slow down abruptly and you to slam on your brakes and inevitably cause all to people behind you to domino effect and follow suit. Thus, creating a traffic jam. Imagine the same scenario but if everyone gave the person space infront of them so that others would be able to maneuver freely to get to their destination, traffic would be non-existent.

It is the space we are allowing ourselves each morning that controls the chaos. If there is no space than there is an increase. Creating space is a great way to manage your life and the world around you. Giving yourself enough time to take a breath and move at a slow and steady, over a racing pace will keep yours and your child's stress levels at a minimum.

If you are a schedule person, then schedule yourself at least 30 minutes each day as a time of reflection whether all together or broken up into segments. 30 minutes to check in with yourself, clear the space, take a deep breath, relax. Restrict yourself from being interrupted during this time. No phone calls, emails, snapchats, etc. You can call them back, know that you are more important than any demands placed on you. With that being said, don't set yourself up for failure and schedule your down time at the busiest hour of the day. Be sure to set a time that works best for you.

My 30 mins is in the morning. I wake up earlier than everyone else in the house to enjoy my 2 cups of coffee (my magic Mom potion) at peace. I thank the Lord for the day and count my blessings, breath in all I am doing right. This sets the stage for a day of success. Satisfied with my thoughts I jump right into preparation for the day. Always be prepared, preparation is Key to success. I iron out and wrinkles in my day, double bookings, etc. then my preparation goes in this order: Me first (always), no its not selfish it's helping yourself before you help others. I get everything I need to be successful in the day. Then my Husband, showing him that I care makes for a happy life and great marriage. Then the kids, lunches, backpacks, breakfast is all a challenge and is extremely time consuming. This alone will suck the energy out of you but if done to the greatest of your ability your successes will trickle down to them. You make sure everyone is dressed, ready, lunch in hand, and looking/feeling amazing. Kiss them all before heading out the door. Expressing love to one another guarantees you all have an awesome day.

It could also go the other way: You then wake up on the defense instead of offence.

Yelling, fighting, frantically finding shoes and backpacks, breakfast on the go, (usually unhealthy) threats are being made if they are not out the door in less than 30 seconds. Baby is crying, and you are running out the door lucky to have your keys and your phone. Lunch was completely forgotten so you are searching the bottom of your purse to find a few dollars and your kid goes to school sugared up with a pocket full of change while you have spilled milk on your back seat. Who can relate to the second scenario?

Our successes as a Mother depend on our preparation. Plan it, provide it, execute it.

When we are making a meal, first we decide what we are having? "Yeah that sounds good" we must get all of the ingredients, "I got this, can't forget this." Then as we lay it out in front of us, we know what it is and what is needed. Now we must put it all together in the correct order to achieve the finished product "meal." Be sure not to neglect it or have the heat (anger) up to high or you will burn it and it will become inedible.

Same with our life. We know what is needed of us on a day to day. Wake up breakfast, clothes, lunches, out the door. Anything we must do to succeed needs to be done ahead of time. Plan 2 days in advance always. If Johnny has karate on Tuesday and Suzie has ballet their uniform & Tutu need to be clean and ready to go Sunday. If you have a big meeting and can't get Johnny to and from soccer, then arrange for someone else to help with the car pool.

Moms, we are in it together we are always willing to help care for another kid and do what we need to do to help simplify each other's lives for we all know how difficult it is being "mother of the year." Don't be afraid to reach out to other moms to share in the care of our little ones. Always make friends with moms on your child sports teams or classes and school. Never be afraid to ask for help but please be respectful of another mom's time. Don't ask last minute and expect great results. In circumstances like this please give a week-3 day notice unless they are your bestie who you can always count on for anything.

Tools:

— Create time and space: 30 mins of "Me" time minimum

— Reach out for help

— Prepare/preplan

CHAPTER 2

Curve ball

Every so often life is going so great. The person in front of you paid it forward at Starbucks and you got a free coffee. Every light was green on the way to work. That co-worker you despise called in sick, your boss catered your favorite lunch. Life feels so good right now. You think to yourself why can't everyday be like this. Then, you get a call from the school nurse saying your kid is throwing up and has explosive diarrhea and you are thinking "Why me" because you know you're going to get it and be out the next 3 days. Yep #Momlife.

Life likes to keep you on your toes and send you curveballs just when you think your life is on the up and up. I could not give you the answer as to why this happens, but I can give you some tools to help ease the pain of the abrupt halt in your perfect day. God likes to send us signs of things we need to do in some very odd and unusual ways. I can't know exactly His plan and reasoning behind it all, but it is up to us to ask for clarity and guidance if a time like this ever takes place in our own life.

God knew that this child was going through a really hard time and needed extra TLC from his wonderful Mother. As she left work and called the doctor for an emergency appointment. She was through the roof upset at the fact the child was sick but by the end of day 2 she knew they both needed a movie and cuddle time to be right with their soul again.

God has a strange way of knowing exactly what you need, it is up to you to be thankful in all circumstances and trusting him to help us throughout tough times.

There was a lady who came up to me and told me her story. Her life was falling apart, she lost her dad, her job, and her house all in the same month. I was thinking how could it get any worst. "Man, that is rough to go through all of that and still be breathing." I said to her. My next question to her was are you surviving or dying? Curveballs are thrown at 100 MPH and sometimes are in the form of a 2 x 4 aiming directly towards your head. I asked her is there anything good in your life? Can you tell me about what is right?

What she is going through is probably the worst pain anyone should have to endure but she could not think of a single thing right with her life. We mourned her father and then I asked her to switch her focus. Reprogram yourself to see the good in the world. Find the right in your life instead of pointing out the wrong. She told me it was hard at first then like the turning of a wheel it was easier and faster to point out the right in life.

This is how depression works, we can no longer find the right and we are focused strictly on what is going wrong. Open your eyes to what is right in life and everything else will fade away. Practice gratitude on a daily and your worries will disappear.

It took her a while to get back on her feet, but she was able to stand again, found a job she loves, and a Man she adores. She has a child who she almost completely lost during this low time. Who is happy and healthy, smart as can be, I know she can make it through. Those tough times are there to make us grow stronger to help us build confidence in ourselves and our actions. Curveballs are given to us to get through times of great need. Sometimes it's a change of perspective, sometimes it's a fulfillment of others. Be vigilant during these times and reach out to the hurting or the needy. Make time to hear God speak to use you in a way to help others for there will always be a time when you are the one that needs the help.

There are lessons to be learned when life hits you hard. Finding out what that lesson is, challenges your mind to widen its scope and think in a design bigger than the world around you. Don't look at the situation, look for the reasoning behind the situation that was placed before you. For if we choose to focus on the situation at hand and never look to the reasoning behind it, the intensity of the curveball grows in rhythm and speed and will beat you down until you have awakened, changed, or given up.

One thing that we can all know, God is always by our

side though each mountain and each curveball. Ask for clarity for all your doubts and "why Me's". Each lesson learned moves you closer to the successes of being a parent. As a child of God, we must go to Him during our time of need as our children come us to find comfort.

Tools:

— Switch your focus

— Find the lesson, not the situation

— Help others in their time of need

— Ask for clarity

CHAPTER 3

Pestered

That moment when you have had enough. You have locked yourself in the closet, hidden with a bag of chips, tub of ice cream and a box of tissues because you have simple had enough. If you hear the word "Mom" one more time you are going to scream. Being a Mom is the most challenging, trivial, wonderful, rewarding thing you will ever do in your life. Just know that you are not alone. You must take your moment to pull yourself together, you deserve a moment. The demands get to much and you just need to get away from it all or you are going to lose it. Do not let them pester you.

A perfect example of being pestered, when that fly keeps

dive bombing you in the face while you are sleeping, and you wake up with a vengeance. You will stop at nothing to get rid of it.

This is what you do with these emotions:

Focusing on the issue will only make the issue worse, you must remove yourself from the situation to restore your sense of normality. Set your kids up with crayons and coloring books (if trustworthy) or a quite puzzle. Just something to entertain them in your absents. Sneak off, if you must tell them you are taking a Mommy moment. Go to your sanctuary.

Now your sanctuary is a place where you can leave all your problems. A place where you can go to relax. If you don't have a Sanctuary, then create one. Mine is a little spot in the back yard that is hidden from the direct view of the house, next to my garden. It always brings calm and serenity and restores my sense of normality. Calms my psycho if you will. Find a place to go, put on soothing music, if your kids are old enough tell them, you need a moment to relax. Please go play quietly in your rooms then we will _____ (fill in the blank) go for a walk, play a game, go to the park, go get ice cream, you name it. It must be something they will enjoy and set up a preconceived consequence. If you need something between now and then get it yourself or wait until I am done or else, we will forfeit our fun. Having the conversation with age appropriate kids 4+ will set your moment up for success.

Now you are ready! Grab a book, drink of your choice, take a well-deserved break from the chaos. Name 3 things your thankful for to refocus your energy. Close your eyes and practice presence, bring your focus to the serenity of the music, the chirping of the birds. Take some deep breathes, the oxygen will help lower the level of cortisol (stress hormone). Don't take too long 30 mins tops or set yourself up for failure. You will return to Johnny threatening to pull off the head of Suzie's doll and Suzie chasing him with scissors and your 2-year-old eating dog food. Nothing we want.

Always keep your promise. The children let you have a moment. It doesn't matter what you came back into prepare yourself for the park, or Ice cream or a walk. Or a walk to the park and ice cream.

Tools:

— Create a sanctuary for yourself
— Have the conversation of what you are doing and what is expected
— Relax – Unwind

CHAPTER 4

Build Trust

Trust, by far is the highest honor. If you are trustworthy you are reliable, admired, confident and you walk with pride. That moment your child loses trust in you their world crumbles. They fall apart emotionally, and it reflects onto every aspect of their life. School, home, friends, vocabulary, this is when the first "I Hate you" comes out. You must build trust within your relationship with your child. Trust, love, communication, and loyalty is the foundation to any relationship. Once trust is broken their life can easily fall. There are a few ways we can prevent this from happening. Simple and easy but detrimental to their beginnings.

Example:

If we say maybe later that is a definite in their mind. They look forward to the later, later comes around you say not today. "Maybe tomorrow?" Tomorrow comes you say you don't have time and they start to fall apart. Take that moment and do what they want. You will achieve a better reaction when you ask them to do things for you. Chores, walk the dog, come here, any request made will have a better response if you adhere to their requests as well. Play a game, child's choice, if you have multiple kids alternate, all must participate. Show interest in your kids and they will aim to please you in every way. Walk around barking orders you will get nothing but defiance in return.

Think of activities to do together, collaborate on ideas, projects, etc. Show interest in growing healthy young adults who can handle their own emotions. Devote time to them before it is too late. When kids are young all they want is your time. You have them 10 maybe 15 short years to instill a good human nature into these little people and then they are grown and off leading their own lives, only reaching out when in need. Raise them to trust others by first trusting you.

Do what they ask of you **always**. Not their demands but their requests, choose to play its good for both parties and you will watch them grow in confidence and pride. Trust is something all people should carry with them. If this sense of trust is broken at a young age it is very hard to repair and as they grow older, they will become untrustworthy themselves. Trust should be held with high reverence and looked upon as wisdom and connection. The moment you realize you told Johnny you would play catch today after school, but you have a meeting with a client either reschedule with your child or make it a quick play session. Roll up your sleeves and give your child 10-15 minutes of your time. Don't just blow them off "sorry champ maybe next time"

Practice Play

It took me months to learn how to play with my first child. He would request me to join in his games and I was always too busy "adulting" to play with him. You are your child's first friend. How you treat them will determine how they treat others. Be mindful of this when you are in the act of play. We must socialize them at a young age by letting them do things with children close to their own age. Supervise and direct their play to keep it positive. The more time they spend with friends the deeper the connection will become. Please do not keep putting him in negative friend situations.

When my child was young, I had coffee with my friend almost every morning, but our boys did not get along. We forced them to play together. This is not a good example of a friendship especially at a young age. Sometimes in life we just don't get along with everyone. Show your child what a good friendship is from the start. Be the first example then be sure to schedule play dates with positive friends to have those good interactions. You will see him start to make connections and come to life.

I was a preschool teacher and witnessed this in many of my kids. It was miraculous every time. They went from being this shy little thing to having confidence and laughing, wanting to learn. True growth happens in positive environments, be the sunshine in your child's life not their rain cloud.

Tools:

— Always choose to play

— Take time for kids

— Connect with your child on their level to build trust

— Get a better result when asking them to do things by really listening to them

CHAPTER 5

Honor their Time

In this digital era, it is easy to lose track of time. 2-3 hours in front of the T.V., phone calls that take you away, texts, social media, snapchat, Pinterest, Instagram, all of these are time suckers. They take you away from the present moment, the moment that really matters. When I was little, I remember asking my Mom to help me with my homework. Back then there was no t-vo or DVR everything was real time and if you didn't watch it you would miss it. She would help me during commercials and leave when her show came back on. So, I would do what I could and wait for her for the rest. Then I would start to play, and she would be back, and I would hop up and go back to my homework 30-minute project took 1 ½ hours.

The Honor system works with kids too.

If you are there when called upon and work with them until the task is completed and set aside other items such as phone and TV it will make them feel like they are important to you, honored. Would you ever answer your phone while in a meeting with your boss? Don't answer the phone while in a meeting with your kid. The moment you answer your phone and walk away is the moment they are left alone needing your help feeling disrespected. Then you come back after talking with your BFF 45 minutes later and they have moved on. The moment is gone, and you try to retrieve it, but it turns into a battle. You have wasted their time and lost their respect. You showed them the phone conversation means more to you than they do, and it leaves them feeling abandoned and hurt.

Solution: Honor your child and their time

Respectfully say "I am so sorry I have to take this call" "Hi Kimmy, Can I give you a call back I'm helping Johnny with this project, yep I will send you pictures, it's going to be amazing. He came up with some awesome ideas, can't wait to show you, okay bye."

This just sent Johnny beaming, he is honored and filled with encouragement and ready to face this project head on until it is complete. He will put in the effort to honor your words of encouragement. "This is going to be an awesome project." At this moment you will see his best effort put forth.

Give them reaction time.

Slow the instant gratification cycle and give them a moment to honor your request. It takes kids a few more moments to wrap up what they are doing and adhere to the demands. Always put urgency on it. I need _____ done immediately then you can come back to what you are doing. Okay play time is over please clean up. Give them a 10-15 second response time before asking again. Put a consequence on the next request that is a few minutes later. See if that will get them moving if still no response, redirect them, then follow through with the consequence. If the television is involved, you will get nowhere. Be sure to turn it off and ask your request again.

Never ask them to do something and walk away with no follow-up this will lead to no follow through with anything. Not a good characteristic to have. We want to raise dependable, responsible, consider it done little human beings. Develop the skill sets within them NOW. You should only have to ask once and they should hop to it. This takes a bit of good training but I have faith you will get there.

Tools:

— Redirect your child do not just talk at them

— Follow-up for the follow through

Skill Set:

— Make them dependable and reliable

— Give them the skills to have a "consider it done" attitude

CHAPTER 6

Accommodations

We Love to make accommodations for people, especially guests. We tell them "make yourself at home, may I offer you a drink, some food?" We try to comfort our guests, welcoming them with open arms. Most of us treat our children the same way. Always accommodating for their needs, wants, and desires.

My son came up to me, he was very young, he said "Mommy, you're my slave."

This statement hit me like a ton of bricks. I realized I do give into his every want, need, and desire never asking for anything in return. I treated him like a prince. Gave into his fits and over compensated leaving me drained, tired, and sometimes frustrated. Something had to change. I will not treat him like a guest anymore or accommodate for his every need, be at his beck and call, come running. I am sure some of you can relate?

We want to do everything for them, ofcourse they are our world. Loving them and doing things for them brings joy to our life. Our job is not to do everything for them. Our job is to train them to become helpful, loyal, honorable, kind human beings and send them on their way. Fully capable of taking care of themselves.

We must set them up for success and give them the skills to mange their own needs.

Step 1: You are not their Slave

If they ask you respond "here let me show you how." Have patience. Learning a new skill takes time and repetition. Yes, it is faster and easier if you just do it yourself but our goal is to train them properly so they can take over the task when ready. After a few times they will be able to get it themselves and it takes a burden off of you.

Step 2: Have them help you.

Have them help with the mundane tasks of the household. If the yard needs tending, ask for help. Laundry, sweeping, mopping ask them to help. My 2-year-old can mop, my 3-year-old loves to vacuum and wipe off counters.

Set them up for success, take the stress off you. If you are working so are they. Let them help you cook. My kids love to bake and be my little kitchen helpers.

Step 3: Celebrate the successes

Let's finish this up and then we will _____ (fill in the blank). Let's clean the kitchen and then we will cuddle up and watch a movie. Once we are finish loading the dishwasher we will have some cupcakes.

Society thrives on awards and children are easily persuaded to do what they must to earn a reward. Since now I was no longer a slave and broke free of my chains my son knows his role within the family and knows what is expected of him. He does most of it without even being asked which has taken stress off me. Everyone in the house should have assigned jobs, from checking the mail, to clearing the table, there is no need for you to do everything. If you have enough helpers delegate out all the jobs, pour yourself a glass of wine and go hide for 20 minutes no longer. Give yourself time and space and a huge congratulations for being a wonderful Mom.

At first it may be a bit challenging especially if you have strong willed children. If your child is strong willed be prepared for a battle. Crying, temper tantrums, every excuse as to why they can't do it/don't want to do it. I hear a lot of "I don't want to" from my 2-year-old. Stay stronger, don't take it off their hands and say "fine, I will do it." If you cave you lose. You might as well just plan on cooking, cleaning, clearing, wiping, loading, filling, and doing everything else while trying to keep your sanity for the rest of their life because they will be living with you. Reality Check it's not going to happen. You will lose your mind sooner or later.

Stick to your guns, stand up tall, and honor your words. 'We don't get ice cream until all of the table is cleared, food is put away, and dishes are done." The first few times they will need redirection but then after a routine is developed it will be like a well-oiled machine, you just need to sit back and listen to it purr in this case watch it run. Forewarning always hold up your end of the bargain. DO NOT LOSE THEIR TRUST. The moment they are all done it is ice cream time.

Tools:

Train your kids

- — Assign daily tasks
- — Define their roles in the family
- — Delegate and take time to reflect and relax

CHAPTER 7

Stick to your Guns

Your child asks you for something you say "No" They cry and whine to get their way and you give in to keep the peace.

NO WAY!!!!!!!! No Thank you. Never again...

You have just lost all power instantly and it is hard to get it back, but not impossible. There is a reason you said no in the first place. You need to trust yourself and stand firm and committed to your gut and don't be swayed by the cries of the little one or big one. As a child, I would stomp and scream, yell and slam doors, and finally my mom had enough she would let me go every time. I carried this "life skill" with me well into my teens. How many times have you seen adult temper tantrums? The stomping around and yelling to get your way is not a correct format to get your point across. As adults we have friendly debates. Teach your child how to debate their opinion out to see if they can persuade you with logical points. If they make a logical effort to present their case and we come to a compromised conclusion then you have won, and they have won. I love win-win situations. You have taught them a positive life skill that they can use the rest of their life to help other coincide with them. Not to flip out when something does go according to his plan.

Have them answer the simple question "why do need _____?"

Ask them to come up with 3-5 reasons why they should do/have what they are asking. If they come up with 3-5 really good reasons as to why they should and you have no red flags as to why they can't, beyond "No." This request should be made before the initiation of the hard "No." If you say no be sure it is a hard "NO" do not say no and then let them go, it is contradictive. If they win the debate put stipulations on the request and adhere to the stipulations.

For example: Johnny wants to go to his friend's house after school tomorrow.

"Honey you have homework."

He says "Timmy and I have a lot of classes together, so we can do it at Timmy's house." "What about dinner?"

"Timmy's mom has already said I could stay for dinner."

"I want you back by 745"

"Yes Ma'am."

"Homework will be done, or you get to clean out the garage and No video games this weekend."

"Thank you Mom, I love you. See you at 745."

Format for the debate:

Base 1 Question? Answer.

Base 2 Question? Answer.

Base 3 Question? Answer.

Home: Consequence - if he does not adhere to the request then you will do…

Always establish the consequence prior to the action so they know exactly what will happen if they disobey you. They should by this point have enough respect and responsibility to be able to handle this. Please do not set your child up for failure. This is a high-level request rebuttal. This child would need to be well established in character and self-discipline. This is the goal we are growing towards.

Since he already knows the consequence and he decide not to keep up his end of the bargain then you must help him clean out the garage and take away the video game console. They will probably flip out but do it anyway. No yelling back at them, do not be angry or upset about it. No "well it told you what would happen" he already knows. When he comes back late with no homework done then say,

"Hi honey, I'm so glad your home. Will you please go check the clock? What time is it?"

"815"

"You are 30 minutes late. Can I please see your homework? Okay sit down here and please do it now. I will be right back to help you. I Love you."

Go directly upstairs and unplug his console and put it where you will be able to see it. Right in the open is fine.

You don't need to hide it. Come back downstairs say nothing and help him with his homework and get him fed if need be, then get him ready for bed. Yes, he may still need help. I tuck my kids into bed well into their teens. It shows them they are important to you still.

They will go into their room and notice the video games are gone and know he needs to do what you ask next time. He will learn when a deal is made then he needs to up hold his end of the bargain. If they know what they did, and you are not mad at them, just follow through with the preset consequence, they will be able to comprehend it without being mad at you or himself. If you start yelling and screaming at him the moment he walks through the door they will not be able to learn from their mistake and next time will be reluctant to come home at all.

If you have little ones you can use this method as well but a little different in procedure.

"Mom, can I have some candy/cookie."

"But sweetheart why do you need the candy; can you give me 3 good reasons?

1. Because you love me
2. Because I love candy
3. I promise to play outside and wash my hands when I am done.

Home: Consequence – no dessert early bed time.

"Okay, please be sure to place the wrapper in the trash and wash your hands. If you don't, I will have to put you to bed early with no dessert."

Teaching your kids how to persuade at a young age will set them up for life skills they will need in the future. Teach it to them young, help them navigate life and they will go through this decision-making process for every move they make.

Don't just say "No" ask them why? Because I said so is not a good answer flip the script and give them control of the situation otherwise, they will walk around with this entitlement that people will do what I say just because I said it. Horrible mind set. To train our kids in this way of thinking will set him up for a lot of fights and broken friendships not to mention a warped sense of reality with bitterness to go along with it. He will have no idea why people don't listen to him or his ideas.

We are growing our children in confidence and affirmation, giving them skill sets for the future.

YOU CAN USE THIS EVERYWHERE WITH EVERYTHING, SO CAN THEY!

Your child will get really good at talking their way out of situations and weighing the pros and cons of every decision. They will go through life asking themselves why the need something over impulsive buying. They will have a better understanding of the way things are and how to get others to see their point of view. Soon you will no longer be able to say no to them because they have already thought about points to rebuttal that you cannot argue with. This is a great life Skill to have and if developed at a young age they will be able to reach great heights in their life and career.

Tools:

— Give me 3 good reasons why I should let you?

— Place consequences prior to giving

Life skills:

— **Persuasion**
— **Responsibility**

CHAPTER 8

Develop a routine

"Success is not just done it is a habit"

Mornings are to be smooth and collected. If you flip out on your kid every morning you increase cortisol levels and the chances for your child to do well in school decrease. Same with you and work. You both become this big ball of stress which leads to being unfocused. To the teacher they are unsupportable and misbehaving, but the truth is it's just the cortisol talking. Every class has that one kid and don't let your child be that kid. When I was growing up, I was that kid, teachers dreaded me and kicked me out of class the first chance they could.

Imagine this, you wake up to a good book (#MIM) and a cup of coffee/tea listen for the birds, take a deep breath of fresh air, thankful for the day. Finish your cup take a nice hot shower. Get dressed and ready the kids walk into the kitchen dressed and ready to go. Pull each one aside to do their hair. You already have lunches packed, shoes are on, backpacks, water bottles, lunches out the door smooth morning.

This never happens. Reality Check: "Johnny where are your shoes?" Suzie is screaming because your trying to brush her hair and jenny just pooped her pants right before you head out the door, your breakfast Is a cold pop tart lunch is 20 different snacks cookies, raisins, apple sauce, etc.… and you are losing your mind.

How do you get from scenario 2 -1? Simple. Prepare and create space. We touched base on this a bit, but I wanted to go more in depth with developing a routine for success in your day to day. The more time allotted = less stress + repetition = morning success.

Instead of staying up until 2 am watching that documentary go to bed with the kids. Read a chapter in a real book (tangible not electronic unless its MIM). Drink some hot tea/glass of wine take a bubble bath. Lower stress first. Your kids will feed off you even though they don't physically feed off you anymore (we hope) they are still tapped into you and react to you. If you are high stress so are, they.

Prepare. Set out clothes the night before backpacks, shoes, dressed head to toes. Get their lunches set out and prepped. So, in the morning all you must do is make 3 PBJ's and put in a milk with an ice pack. Have water bottles clean and ready. Set up your coffee maker so all you must do is press a button. Clean the kitchen the night before and run the dishwasher. Prepare everything you possible can the night before. There is no need to scramble in the morning. Our kids are young eggs their yolks are very sensitive.

Set your kids and yourself up with a routine. Suzie bathes in the morning while Johnny and Jenny take baths at night. Give kids at least 60-90 minutes to get ready give yourself double that. I like to give myself 2 ½ hours for extra space to clear my mind. That is an hour for you, an hour for them, 30 minutes to get out of the door. If there is a special event always preplan a day or 2 ahead of time or arrange for things to change, prepare the kiddos as well. They love routines, and some do not do well if the routine changes abruptly without warning.

On Wednesday, "now remember you are going to Grandma's to stay so whatever you want to bring be sure to pack it." Give them each a bag. The day before checking their bag and help them procure all necessities. We would hate to get a call that blankie is not in the bag and Jenny is screaming the whole time and your Mother refuses to watch them more than one day. Ruining all future weekend getaways.

School and vacations are 2 high stress situations. When we went on vacation my parents were freaking out hours prior to our departure. My sister would go hide in the car, so she didn't have to hear it and my brother would put on head phones to drown out the sound. I was the oldest, so I was expected to help. It was a nightmare. Dad would pack the same day, Mom was up all night and all of us left hungry, so we would stop and get something to eat on the way out. Taco bell before a 15-hour car trip was never a good idea.

Thus, preparation is key to developing a routine and let this become a habit for a better lifestyle for you and your kids.

Tools:

— Create time and space in the morning – 2 ½ hours to get ready.

— Prepare the night before

— Vacation: start packing 2- 3 days prior.

— Check children's bag for necessities

CHAPTER 9

Momster

That moment when you are fuming. Steam is coming out of your ears, face all red, top blows off, starting to yell like Donald Duck flipping out and no one understands a word you are saying. They try to walk away but end up in tears. "I just cleaned up this mess. Why would you do that? Really? Really? I can't believe you right now."

"You know better" "How dare you"

Any of these sounds familiar? Don't act like this has never happened.

That Moment you go "oh no, I sound like my Mother." Welcome to your "Momster Moment."

Your kids don't listen, everyone is yelling, screaming,

hitting, fighting, slamming doors, stomping around and all you want to do is be in a clean house and have kids who are well behaved and listen. here's how you do it.

1. Respect:

If they don't respect you, nothing you say will change anything, no matter how many times you ask them you will never produce the positive outcome. Change your tone to have control of yourself first rather than of others. Use a tone that is comprehensive and doesn't put them on defense. "Suzie will you be Mommy's big helper and pick up your shoes off the floor, so we don't trip over them?"

Instead of:

"How many times have I told you not to leave your shoes in the middle of the floor pick them up NOW."

Onc makes the kid feel like a Rock Star super helper, the other makes her feel worthless, like scum of the earth, one will have a positive reaction while the other a negative. Do you get my drift? Are you picking up what I am putting down?

If we speak to our kids in positive tones, we in turn will obtain a positive reaction and feel positive. We uplift our children and ourselves. This isn't the easiest but it is the best method to earning your child's respect and getting the reaction we are looking for. Teach your child by setting the example. Yelling at them teaches them to yell. Control of self isn't easy either.

You just walked up stairs to search for your grandma's recipe for her snickerdoodle cookies, Suzie wandered into the kitchen and pulls down the tub of flour. When you walk back in it is everywhere and you just mopped. Go ahead scream, yell, throw her in timeout. You will be mad the rest of the evening. Tell everyone about it, cussing while you clean the mess and Suzie feels like the worst human being on this planet wishing she was never born.

-Or-

…You take a deep breath and find a place of love within yourself. Get down on Suzie's level and say, "oh my what a mess you made." She smiles, and giggles covered in flour and you let her play while you use this picture op and post it immediately. You wipe down the counters sweep it into a pile and start writing her name in the flour. When play time is done, sweep up the mess and put Suzie in the bath. "Okay let's not do that again it was a big mess" she nods her head in agreement. You call your husband and ask him to stop to get more flour, so you can bake the cookies. Telling Suzie "this is what the flour is for silly."

The role we play in our child's life is who they grow up to become. I have played both roles and still struggle with this strategy creating the space in your life will lessen your "Momster moments" and it will soon become natural to approach the situation in a calm manner. If you are short fused, your child will be the same way. Don't let everything set you off. Take time for yourself and practice self-love. Learn to control your emotions, think before you react, and always react in a positive way. You show your kids kindness and love they will show each other the same.

2. Monkey See Monkey Do

If you fly off the handle every time something goes obscured, then expect the child to do the same when they don't get their way. Every time they ask you to do something and you don't immediately accommodate their needs expect a meltdown.

How do we fix this?

Practice self-control.

Having control of one's emotions is a great coping mechanism that will be cherished in the future. Identifying what emotion is being felt and how to properly handle that said emotion. There is a good way to handle the emotion and a negative way. We must develop constructive ways to handle our own emotions to show our kids to do the same.

Positive VS. Destructive

Let them know it's okay to be mad but slamming things around and yelling is not the best way to express this emotion, yet it is the most common. In the diagram below you have the emotion and positive ways to express that emotion. It is not okay to wright off your child's emotions.

Use these tools to help them cope with their own emotions and you can use them as well.

Coping Mechanisms	
Being sad	Create - Craft Be around people you love/love you Hugs
Angry	Exercise Run, go to a park, go on a walk, swim Deep Breathe Give yourself space - reflection
Hurt	Physical touch Sleep Self-care

There is a positive way of handling your emotions. Always reach towards the positive nature over what comes naturally. It is easy to think, act, and feel negatively. Use positive coping mechanisms to practice self-control. Show your children you are in control and it is okay to feel but it is not okay to harm and destroy.

Always express your emotion from a place of love.

Practicing love for self and control of self is a great start to show our kids that they too can be in control of their own emotions as well.

CHAPTER 10

Family time

Family time is quality time.

Children thrive on quality time. How many times a day do you hear, "Do you want to play _____ with me?" How many times do we say "No" because we are too busy being an adult?

"Sorry babe, I'm cooking dinner, cleaning, Mommy's on the phone. They interpret these as excuses on why we can't spend time with them doing what they want us to do.

Monkey see monkey do. "I need you to pick up your toys"

"Sorry Mommy, I can't my leg hurts…my tummy hurts, I need water, etc.

Sound Familiar?

The next time you are asked to play, play. Stop your conversation "Sorry Nikki I have to call you back." Watch your child light up. Don't wimp out 2/3 of the way and modify the play to accommodate your needs. The play needs to be interactive on their level not brought up to yours. You need to take your adult mind out of the situation and find your inner child. The more you do it the longer you will be able to sustain the fun. Be silly, let go, have fun, and play with your child. You will be her first friend, his first love, and their Mom forever. Build the friendship when they are young. Don't just drag him around doing only what you want him to do. Let him choose sometimes too. Don't just take him to a jump park (trampolines) and stay on the side lines looking at your phone, plan to play together. A family that plays together stays together.

Family Game Night.

After dinner a few nights a week we play games together. Yes, we have dinner together, we put away the phones, then clear the table together, and play games together. We take turns choosing the game and always adhere to the request, even pie in the face. Start it and keep it going, you may hear some grumbling at first but it will subside after a few times of fun. Be sure to make it fun. No one likes game night when one person calls all the shots, shouting out cheater and storms off. Keep the mood light and don't emphasize so much on playing the game right it's about the time spent together.

Do not be a fun sucker. If you play and always win

then others won't want to play. If you flip out when you are winning and start bad mouthing everyone, no one will want to play. If you keep checking the rules saying you can't do that, no your wrong. No one will want to play. Do not let the competition of the game get in the way of the family fun. In order to keep the atmosphere light rules are explained at the beginning and everyone must follow the same rules and kindly correct them if need be, explanation is useful and not demeaning. Do not start arguing over where Suzie should move her piece, she does have a small advantage due to the fact of she is still learning. Learning takes time, patience, and stability. Provide the right kind of atmosphere for fun. Not just competition, especially when they are young.

Family Movie night

It is sometimes challenging to agree upon a movie that everyone wants to see. Always refresh the movie selection and have agreeance to what they want to watch. You will have some favorites that you will show over the course of months but do not do it often. If you have movie night every night it is no longer a special thing and can have adverse effects. Be sure that they know a routine with movie night. Give plenty of time to show the movie picked, not to close to their bed time. Do not let movie time take away their bed time routine.

My family and I always do our movie nights on Friday and once every 3 months we go out to the theater to see a new release. More if there is something the whole family wants to see. But we have developed a routine. We make dinner earlier, clean the kitchen, then everyone runs off to grab pillows and pajamas. We cuddle up with some popcorn and dessert. Once we are all together then we have commenced Family Movie night. My husband and me are cuddled up with a child under his arm and a child under mine and our oldest is stretched across our legs. We are sure to have some sort of physical touch with all of the children so we are connected. This part makes family movie night one of the best.

We honor each other's time by pausing if there is a drink or potty break. It makes them feel important. We wait for their return and it helps everyone get all the wiggles out while we wait.

Family Activities

The more we do together the tighter our family will become. We include everyone and let each child achieve a success. If its going to the park and playing soccer, frisbee, you name it. We do it together. If one kids goes to the park we are all at the park and me and my husband are right there along side with them on the jungle gym. We go to games and activities for each child and support them in their learning and growth. I keep my kids active, this gives them less room for destruction.

Check out what your local recreation center has to offer for classes. I have my kids in swimming, gymnastics, skating, lego classes, you name it. Always signing them up for fun activities and I do a few classes myself. You need to be sure to grow and learn with your family, leave the kids with your husband and go take a yoga class, or whatever suits your interest. Be sure your husband does the same. Stay active and you will be able to have more fun in general.

Coming together as a family and enjoying/congratulating each other on their success helps develop relationships between the children and brings you closer.

Tools:

— Set time aside for family

— Stay active – classes/ learning opportunities

— Celebrate each other successes - Support

CHAPTER 11

Respect

Watch what you say, watch what you show, watch what you do for they will mimic you. You now have a little mini me and you give them the words of their vocabulary. Everything they say and do has come from you or the people in their life. Make sure the vocabulary you are giving them is one you want them to have, give them words that show respect by practicing it yourself. If you show disrespect on a regular basis, they will do the same. You can't demand a childs respect for they are only acting or speaking upon what has been shown. They learn from you. The yelling, spanking, telling them "NO" all the time. "No" is the one of a childs top 5 first words spoken for it is the word spoken the most. Show them how you need them to behave. Be slow to anger, calm and collected. Talk to them and listen, show them what to do and how to make better choices.

The respect starts with you. Self-control will help you regulate the level of respect you have toward yourself and others. Self-love is another great way to be respectful. Smile at others and do your good deeds and show your kids how to serve others. Find something to do that you love and have enough respect for yourself to always do it.

Do not let your child tell you "No."

You need to start this discipline at a young age. It begins as soon as they can talk so limit the word No from your vocabulary. Un-ah is a big one for me. If you must say No, then replace it with "No thank you" it puts respect into a very disrespectful word.

Please never use the word "dumb" in my opinion this is also a very disrespectful, nasty word that comes out of children's mouths too often. I replace this word with "silly." "Oh, honey will you please stop acting so silly right now." The moment you say "Stop being so dumb" it diminishes their character beyond comparison.

Never use the word "shut-up" when it comes back you will be infuriated. I would replace it with the word "Silence" or "please be quiet, it is not time to talk" or "can we please lower our voice it's a bit too loud for me."

Always ask your child for manners. If you submit to their demands, they lose respect for you. If you adhere to their requests you gain mutual respect: "Give me a glass of water" or "can I, please have a glass of water?" "Thank you for your manners of course you can have a glass of water" If they don't use it properly request them to ask you appropriately until they start doing it on their own.

Do Not let them talk rude to you or others and vice-versa. Remember you give them all the words they say.

"Get out of the way", "Move" or "will you please excuse me?"

"Give me that", "No that's mine" or "Can I please have that back?" "Thank you Ma'am"

We must teach our children respect by being respectful to them first. Yes Ma'am, No ma'am, yes sir, no sir, please, thank you, your welcome and excuse me. These are all words you need to administer into your vocabulary immediately and over use them. Instill these in your child and they in turn will become very respectful.

When your child has no respect for you, you will hear them say the worst things just to hurt your feelings. This is not what it seems. It is a cry out for help they are pleading with you to be kinder, more loving, and compassionate. Care for their needs and desires more often. You hear them being nasty to you but, they are hurting from you. Instead of back lashing and firing back battling with your child simply say, "I'm sorry you feel that way." Keep your composure and give them a hug they may try to resist you. You just told them that you have my attention I am listening, what do you need from me on an emotional level to stop hurting?

This hurt will lead you to fights at school, ending up with the wrong crowd, and down a very self-destructive path. No parent wants that.

It's time to switch tracks quick speak to his emotions. Spend time and build up his ego a bit. Make him feel loved and appreciated. Make his day by doing his favorite thing, let him know how special he is and that he means the world to you. Let him lash out if he needs to, do not leave him alone. Ask him to join you for a walk to release the anger appropriately.

CHAPTER 12

Choices

We are big on giving kids choices. Explaining exactly what their options are plus the consequences involved equaling the follow through of the already preset consequence if the agreement was not met. This equation sets a foundation for discipline. Your choices are A or B if you choose neither than your consequence will be C.

Example:

You can either sit down or go to the corner but if you keep throwing a fit and stomp around than you will go to your room and have no Tv/phone/iPad for 3 days.

The consequence must be reasonable and affect them enough to change the desired behavior. We are looking for positive results that don't require a lot of force to correct their action. No throwing out weeks/Months it just makes them feel like your flexing your power to much and will make them more likely to become deceptive. Plus, it is difficult on you to follow through for lengthen amounts of time.

Giving them choices makes them feel like they have some power. Also helps strengthen their decision-making skills. This life skill can be used positively in the future. Give your child choices, adhere to those choices don't, once again, flex your power muscle and veto their choice. Go with it.

This is a give and take relationship you must remember to compromise on a regular basis. But all within moderation. Do not always give them an opinion. Let them know the plan and if they behave then they can be rewarded with an activity of their choosing. Example: First we are going to the bank, stopping by Nannas, grocery shopping then, if you are good and if weather permits it, Ice cream, the park, and a family game of your choosing. 3 strikes you're out. If you need to be redirected to many times you will lose the fun things to do for you. Always give them a few chances. Second warning, there goes Ice cream, 3rd there goes ice cream and park. If they still think your words mean nothing, then after dinner, bath and bed time, no games. Next time they will remember, oh no I better listen to mom and behave. If you give in and tell them no ice cream and give them ice cream your words mean nothing.

Tell the kid we have a lot to do we will do a few things for me and a few things for you. The expectation set is for you act like a well-behaved child and don't freak out because I won't give you a sucker or a cookie at the store. Pre-set expectations and consequences. Help them know the rules and any foreseen speed bumps. Explain everything to them so they have control over the events ahead of them and know what is happening. If you know Suzie loves the pet store right next to the grocery store and you usually go there for a few moments before shopping tell Suzie that we will not be able to go to the pet store today, but we will go soon when we have more time. Avoid the break down of Suzie asking to go and you saying No and then listening to her cry the whole entire time in the store, so you stop by for a bit to calm her tears. Big speed bump. Eliminate the questions and frustrations along with anxiety for the child who is just along for the ride. Answer all foreseen requests and enjoy the smooth ride.

Once a week/month let them choose a dinner, get them involved. My children love to help me cook/bake. My son is great at cracking eggs and chopping vegetables. My Girls love to pour and stir. This helps them with their creativity and make them feel like they accomplish/contribute to cooking together as a family. Compliment them on the delicious food they made and thank them for a job well done. This will be a life skill they will use forever. Start young, my 2-year-old can stir, add ingredients. Anything you do, do it together.

Tools:

— Let them decide on what they want to do, giving them options gives them power

— Let them help

— Give them the knowledge of what you are doing to prepare them for the future

Life Skill:

— Making Positive choices

CHAPTER 13

Encourage VS Tear Down

You are a mirror reflection of your children. They learned everything from you. Remember that the next time something nasty and mean comes out of their mouth. If your kids are fighting and are rivaling for your attention chances are there is a favorite child or a new baby that never gets in trouble. Babies are attention suckers. You may see that your other child will start acting out. This is a cry for help, encourage him instead of tearing him down. Make him feel loved and uplift their spirit. Encourage them to do right. Ask them to be your big helper and it will give him pride in being an older sibling. I have done it first hand, playing with the baby then yelling at my other kid. Totally inappropriate. Don't always point out their flaws, emphasize on the good things they do. Children are very susceptive on how they are treated. Honor them with kindness show them how you want them to act with your words and actions. Upscale it to make them feel special. "Oh wow, you drew a picture for me, thank you so much I love it, great job." React in this manner and they will love to bring you presents. Remember they are your mini-me and you must be careful on how you act towards them. They do what you do.

You scream, they Scream. You slam doors, they slam doors. You hit them, they hit each other. When raising multiple kids, it is easy to lose control and wanting to get it back by force. Not always the best method. We must teach them we can get our point across without yelling. All the yelling does is let them know you have lost control. You yell they cry, and their cry out vocalizes your yell, so they win. It is a loose-loose battle.

Control your own emotions and stop yelling:

I can't believe you You did this again How many times have I told you? You know better How dare you	Wow, sweetheart Please don't touch this We have talked about this before I will trust that you will not do this again Honey, No thank you!

One way kills the child on the inside and yourself. The other promotes caring, understanding, and forgiveness. Teaches them the life skill of learning from your mistakes.

Always have them respond to you with respect. Ask for it, give them the words.

"Yes Ma'am"

"Yes Mommy"

The Box Method

Frustration levels are high you are on the verge of pulling out your hair or running upstairs to lock yourself in a room to cry or to stop you from doing something you will regret. You are thinking at this moment, why in the world would anyone ever have kids? You want to give them the world but the more we give the more they take. We are left used and abused with nothing left but a stump. What happens when you have nothing left to give, they chop you down and sit on you.

This can lead you to so many different emotions and we tend to lash out on our kids. The problem is they don't know what they are doing, they instinctively go until they cannot go anymore, and they turn around and start heading the other way. Have you ever chased a running toddler? The moment you have them cornered they turn around laughing and keep running. It is up to us to set our boundaries.

The Box Method

Emotional

Physical

Mental

Special

This concept is set in place with consistency and discipline

These are the boundaries set and if consistent, will keep your kids from driving you nuts. I am warning you now, consistency is the key to this method. Let them get away with it once you might as well throw in the towel and surrender all control.

Once a child is contained and all their needs are being met within the box parameters they will grow. They will grow mentally, physically, emotionally, and specially. It's like putting a plant in a pot, transplanting. If the pot is to big the plant dies, to small and it doesn't grow. Perfect size and the plant thrives, along as other needs are being met. Like water and sunlight, consistency and discipline.

Emotionally: Are all their emotional needs being met or are they an emotional wreck?

Our children are very sensitive to the emotions within and around them. We must develop adversity within our children and sprinkle them with love and encouragement to help them grow. Support their needs and let them explore the world. Do not be overly protective. Give them opportunities to learn from mistakes. When hurt do not overly coddle them. Tell her your Ok brush it off. If they need you let them walk over to you (dependent on the situation). Help them to know they are loved and all is well. Do not let your emotions spill over into them. They should not have adult worries at all. Give them a sense of security and hope for the future.

Physically: Support their movements and challenge them.

All kids are the best at something. My son is very physical, my daughter very emotional. This is a skill that can be worked on. Help support them with their physical growth. Give them tasks that are their level difficult. When at the playground continue to play with them. Be active, play catch, soccer. Help them develop physical skills. Some kids it comes naturally others they will have to work on it.

Mental: Give them problems to solve.

Children are too often are sat in front of the television offering them over stimulation. Not good for brain development. We need to move away from the tech-stimulants and back to physical realm stimulants. Practice math, writing, reading with your child. Read to them every day. Help them to read. Developing a love for reading at a young age will set them on a good path. Mental work will help them become strategic thinkers. Support their need for learning. Sit down with them help them color or write their name. Give them problems to solve while driving. Point out words on a building to read, street signs, etc.

Special: Make your children feel special.

Give them your time and do nice things for them. Give little things to show your love, notes in their lunchbox, hugs in the morning, special breakfast. Let them know that you cherish them and are happy they exist. Fill your child with Joy for they are your world. They need to know that. I am always hugging, kissing and loving on my children. I do not over use the words I love you but I do show it on a constant basis. I will have care packages ready for them after school and plan dates for each child so we can have quality time. My husband does the same. He will be sure to have that special time with each child and do a project together to get them all involved.

While we do want to develop our children mentally, physically, emotionally, and specially we need to set boundaries with consistency and discipline. If I am always hugging on my children and let them do practically anything they want then they will become entitled. Never giving back or contributing. If I develop great math and computer skills but do not get her outside to play catch then she will become a hobbit. If my child is great at playing ball and very active but every time he doesn't catch the ball he has a mental break down he will become an angry player and a sore loser, trash talking everyone all the time. Our goal is to be consistent with each boundary set and discipline when needed. If all Suzie wants to do is color and get hugs it is time to put on some discipline and get her active and play catch. If Johnny wants to play catch all the time you need to show some discipline and get him inside hitting the books. This should not be a battle. If done consistently they will be able to easily transition between each activity without a meltdown. Growing their emotional security. Growing mentally, physically, emotionally, and specially with discipline and consistency.

Tools:

— Consistency and Discipline
— Choices

Life skills:

— mentally, physically, emotionally, and specially secure
— Learn from your mistakes

CHAPTER 14

Collaboration

While consistency is key it may be difficult if you have different views of raising children. Make sure all parties of authority are collaborating in order to provide consistency needed for the stability of your child. Most children are being raised in a "broken" home. Let me explain that term, it doesn't mean anything is wrong with it. "Broken" is a term that I am going to use as anything other than a Mother figure and Father figure in the home. If there are grandparents in the home than we need to have this conversation. Aunts, Uncles, roommates, anyone who helps care for the child. Everyone needs to work together to provide the same ground rules. This may prove difficult in split custody battles where this is no conversation without gnashing your teeth but, it is still encouraged.

The conversation needs to include 5 things:

1. Set goals

You want them to be responsible. Give them jobs to do around the house. Don't over work them, use age appropriate things for them to do. Ask that this is reinforced. Have your child help with setting goals. Becoming goal oriented at a young age is a great skill. We are building skills for life and I am sure if you explain in this way to all parties in your Childs life they would love to contribute.

2. Set rules/boundaries

Have each household state the rules. Make them clear don't expect the child to know, then get mad at them when they cross the invisible line. Kids are very adaptable and can only go off what they get away with unless stated otherwise. Make it crystal clear for them and remove all the guess work. This is for everyone grandparents, aunts, uncles, step parents, anyone who spends a significant amount of time with the child. Please don't let the list be too long and specific. Just set guidelines. 3-5 good rules.

3. Create a safe space for your child

Just like adults like having a living room to hang out, so do your kids. Create a space besides their room. Even if it is small, maybe a rug with a chair and a basket of toys/bookshelf. This is great in building responsibility. You may set boundaries and expectations with this area. Make them responsible, they must keep it clean, picked-up and organized. Be sure to reward them for their efforts. Simple praise such as great job works well.

4. Let them have a voice

Sometimes you can overrule them but in order to raise confident children we must listen to them. With so much technology draining our attention it is almost a battle the child must fight every day. "Daddy come play" "Sorry bud, Daddy is busy" "Mommy can we go to the park?" "Sorry baby Mommy's on the phone" They have been silenced and then adhere to video games.

5. Be on the same page

Collaborate to have consistency with all parties. Everything will not be the same just some basic rules. No candy before dinner, No T.V before school, homework, reading before bed, etc. Keep it all simple and easy to remember and follow for your child and others. Once ground rules are set your child will not cross the line. They will be sure to tell others they cannot cross the line.

Tools:

— Consistency

— Have the conversation make it simple and clear

— Set simple rules to follow for all

CHAPTER 15

Deciphering the cry's

Children cry for many reasons. When they are born, we get good at knowing what they need by the tone of their cry. As they get older, we need to pay closer attention to the cries. They need you forever and you will always need to be aware of their needs (without dismissing yours). Our children will never say what they need and what they are asking for is usually the opposite of what they are needing. If they say they are fine, it is probably a sign that they are not fine, especially if they are yelling it at you. We need to always come to them with compassion and loyalty. Just being a silent rock in a time of need may be enough to calm the storm rolling within. As an infant it was easier to provide for their needs. Clean diaper, fed, burped, sleep, physical contact. Easy. As they grow into their teens their needs change so dramatically there is an infinite list of items that could be going on with them all at the same time. Develop a method to help them get through these tough times in life. Remember you are their safe place during these troubled times don't react to their action just be their safe place. If you are being yelled at don't ever yell back. It is a sign they are hurting. If they are crying, they are hurting, and emotional hurt is the worst. Don't expect an answer just let them work through the pain and help them to reestablish themselves. Support them in their time of need, be a rock. Strong and silent. Make everything is Ok and let it be known they are wonderful and you are proud.

There are many different cries and as they get older the list gets longer and is harder to decipher what they are needing and how to help the situation. There are many times where there is literally nothing you can do. At a certain age they start to shy away from you affection and it could be trivial to even hug on them. Fight through the push away and break down their protective wall build by their pain. Show them you do care and still love them as much as you have always loved them from day 1. Do not let their anger make you turn away and leave them to deal with the emotional storm within. Hear their cry for help:

our main cries:

To get their way	Negative cries need corrective action
Cry for help	Positive cry needs your attention and love
Cry for attention	Positive – just a hug will help and a listening ear.
Pain	Positive in need of compassion
Cry to Alert you (reaction based)	Negative needs to be ignored. This cry needs to be reconciled.
Cry for needing something	Positive could be emotional or physical. Needing to fulfill all the physical needs and then you can fill the emotional.

You do not need to emotionally react for every cry. Decipher if it is a positive or negative cry as to what kind of reaction is needed to take place. Teaching them independence will lessen the cries. Let them do things for themselves to become a big helper, don't do it all for them. Be there for support and a shoulder to lean on will be enough. If they are yelling and hurt do not yell back and teach that we must argue our way through life. Teach them that you are allowed to be emotional but we need to express our emotions in manners that are productive and not destructive.

Tools:

— Recognize a cry for help and hurting
— Decipher what kind of reaction is needed
— React to your child with love and understanding

Life Skill:

— Handle emotional turbulences

CHAPTER 16

Bed Time Battle

Mommy I am...thirsty, hungry, 5 more minutes please, every excuse in the book. They will go down the list if you give them the chance. Persistence and consistency = success. Do not let this vary to much we are human in nature, creatures of habit, develop a routine that best fits your little ones. Make it the same every night and don't let it slide just because its Friday or the Weekend. Keep it the same routine each night and your kids will stop fighting you.

Here is what I do: I put my girls (2-4) to bed first, while I send my son (7) to go get ready. We all grab our waters and all head upstairs, brush our teeth, Pj, pick out a story. My son reads to the girls then he says goodnight and I sing to the girls we say our prayers. He picks out a book for me to read to him and crawls into bed. I read him a story and say our prayers and sing our songs. Each child has their own list of favorite bed time songs and I be sure to take their requests as they sing with me. I tuck in each child into their own bed, give them a kiss, give them their stuffed animals, special blanket and turn off the lights. Each one has their moment and their time to know that they are loved.

I do give special treatment to my oldest. He needs more one on one centered attention because I need him to be a rock for these girls and if he is at all hurting, he will take it out on them first. I show him he is loved, is special, near, and dear to my heart. He has his book ready, one for him, one for me and I do not keep him waiting too long. We have story time, sing our special songs that are just for him. Kiss him goodnight, tuck him in. I have wonderful sleeping babies all night long.

This scenario is played out night after night and has taken years of practice in developing the routine with them. If I forget something, they are quick to let me know. Don't deny them of what they are needing it will only backfire with restless nights. If they want 20 pillows to meet their comfort needs, then give them the 20 pillows. Do not turn bedtime into a battle. I know my kids and what they need in order to sleep peacefully. I feed into their wishes, so I can have a restful night sleep. Otherwise you in turn get no sleep and neither does your child and both of you are irritable and restless.

Every child is different, play into their individuality to develop a sense of security and safety associated with their bed. Your bed is your refuge not a battle field. Even as adults we have a bedtime routine. I wash my face, brush my teeth, put on my Pjs, get a glass of water, read my book, write in my journal, say my "I am" Mantras, kiss my husband goodnight, crawl into bed, say my prayers, tuck my 5 pillows around me and cover up with my 2 blankets. This gives me my sweet dreams. I must have most of this, in this order, every evening in order to get the best night sleep I can. If I don't there is no sleeping for me. Same goes for your child.

Tools:

— Give in to their requests
— Help them Love their bed

Life skills:

— Routine
— Security
— Good Sleep

CHAPTER 17

Corrective Action (CA)

"A low toned stern voice works better than a yell."

Have you tried everything? Spanking, yelling, standing in the corner and that child of yours just won't listen. Nothing works! You are stumped.

"How do I get these kids to listen to me?"

The answer: Become their best friend. If they enjoy you and your company, they will want to please you by doing the requests you ask of them. You are from birth their only friend and you show them what friendship means play games with them, teach them. It is easy when they are infants. It seems like you are constantly playing with them and teaching them things. Holding and kissing them all over, celebrating successes. It stops when they reach about 2 when you tell them No 200x a day. If you continue playing games, teaching them to share, help them and they will want to help you.

You may say "I am not their friend I am their parent."

That is when the low toned stern voice comes into play. Simple statements like "Johnny, No thank you." These words place respect in the relationship over control.

Once you have befriended them and do as they ask cheerfully and to the greatest of your ability. Not becoming their "Slave" just playing games and spending quality time with them their ears are open to you. The moment you start yelling they close them again. Literally covering their ears.

You may need to yell in a group to get their attention but quickly bring your tone back down to ask your request. Once the request is made give them reaction time. Kids move very slow, it takes them a few moments to register and get their body to move the way you asked them. Follow-up 2-5 minutes later If they have not moved, then set in the consequences. If you are needing immediate results, then state the urgency. Do not request something then follow-up with a yell it does not make them want to listen to you. Ask and then have them answer with a "yes Mama" and send them off to adhere to the request. This can be used during sibling fights, not listening, asking multiple times. This method puts you back in charge.

Most parents now a days are being overrun by their kids because parents don't know how to discipline and are more likely to give up and let the child take the reins. This is never a good idea. CA is needed immediately. Taking back control will be hard. One of the hardest things you will do, but your children need to understand that you are here to navigate them and you have rules and expectations you want them to follow. Set some simple ground rules and help them follow with redirection.

Example:
1 Clean up after yourself
2 Put on your listening ears
3 Keep your hands, feet, and words kind

Remind them which rule they broke and let them know you mean business.

For CA to work you must first befriend them adhere to their requests. I am not talking about going to McDonalds every night or watching the same movie over and over. I mean going outside and playing catch, soccer, going to the park, and participating not just sitting on the bench watching your phone. Sit down with them and color or read stories, as many as they want to read. Quality time requests.

Once you have spent the time with them and invested yourself into play you both will grow in your relationship. It will be difficult but soon you will be using your imagination along side them and both of you will flourish.

Tools:

— Say it with me, "A low toned, stern, voice works better than a yell." Mom means business when she gets quiet.

— Quality Time requests – always choose to play

— Redirect your child do not just talk to them

— Give them reaction time

CHAPTER 18

Big helper

From the time that your child can walk they can help. Give your children tasks, it is human nature we have a desirable need to have a purpose. We must contribute towards the success of the family. Give them tasks that are manageable and challenging, let them clear the table and help with the dishes. My simple rule of thumb, if you are cleaning, they are cleaning. DO NOT DO IT FOR THEM. Sure, it is easier for you to do it and then you won't have to hear them whine at all. But we are teaching life skills not if you complain enough you won't have to do anything.

We grow from the struggle then we can celebrate the success. Give your child difficult (for them) tasks and then rejoice with them. Have them help with groceries, cooking, laundry, cleaning, mopping, vacuuming, the more they do for the family and contribute the less entitled and bratty they will act. You may have to battle at first "I don't want to" "No" "Can't you just do it" Stand your ground, fight through it. Please do not forfeit and do it for them. Redirect them if you must but it will get easier with repetition. Do Not just talk at them. "I told you do this, do it now" Ask once then get them and direct their attention to the task requested of them. This does not mean grab them and drag them to get it done. There should be no tear shed. Supervise and assist of needed until the task is complete. DO NOT let them walk away from an incomplete task that you have to drag them back to it. This means you were not being attentive. Stick with them until the task is complete then reward them by letting them do what they want while you finish up dinner. We are building life skills: Complete the task given to you.

CHAPTER 19

Be Thankful

Each day you are fighting a battle. Teaching your child right from wrong, while keeping it all together ourselves. You end up just battling your child to prove you are right this never turns out good. The moment you have won the battle your child is in tears and left wounded and you are filled with anger and regret. Always end the argument with love and compassion, surrender the cause and use it as a pivot point to grow.

A seed planted must push (fight) its way to the surface to break ground to grow toward the sun. Too much sun will burn up the plant. Let your love flow like water, too much will rot the seed, hints spoiled rotten. You need the right amount of Love and sternness to develop confidence within your child. Help them bloom with positive reinforcement, shade them from harm, attend to any weeds (bad behavior) Correct it with redirection, breath in Oxygen (gratitude) breath out stress (need for control)

Breathe in Love
Breathe out anger

Breathe in Happiness
Breathe out hate

Fill yourself with joy and Love and you will be able to disperse it. Complain and nag all day long and you will also disperse it. Your children in turn will complain about everything.

Your children reflect you, be thankful for what you have. An attitude of gratitude creates a happy heart, it heals the pain, releases the anger. Name 3 things that make you happy and 3 things your thankful for, have your kids do the same. This disrupts the negative thinking pattern. Do it every night, get more in depth with your thanks.

Example:

I am thankful for the life change that has developed an opportunity for me to expand my knowledge and disperse it among the nations helping people around the world become kinder parents and raising kinder children to better the next generation of people on the planet.

I started with this method "I am thankful for…" and it changed my life. Being thankful switches your thought process. At first it is difficult to even think of one thing but with practice you will find more and more to be thankful for. Practice with your kids. Have them name 3 things they love about their life.

Reward system: Incentives

My son is amazing. Absolutely wonderful but, he sometimes does not have his listening ears turned up. This becomes a big problem. If I must ask more than once it becomes a problem. Imagine 15-20 years from now his teacher asks him something or his Boss and he just ignores them since he never developed his listening skills at a young age. He would be a heavy liability. Let's turn our kids into assets and ensure their future is smooth sailing with the consider it done attitude. Be sure to redirect your child if they are not listening. Do not ask 2-3-5 times. Just once, then gently push them in the right direction. So perfect example. I asked my child to get ready for bed. I have gone above and beyond as to write out his routine in a place where it is seen and can be reference i.e. bathroom mirror. He is playing when I asked him to get ready. Toys were then gone. I asked once and then he did not acknowledge the request or only did it half way. My Father always told me to not half #$@ things so I am trying to teach my son the same morals with some different verbiage.

He threw the biggest fit. Screaming crying, I stayed calm and simply said are you ready for bed? He of course said "yes" So we went down the list together and he was missing a few items on that list. I gave him a chance to earn his toys back. If you do this then you will get this. So, if you get up and are totally ready without me asking you multiple times to get ready, I will give you your toys back, Deal?

He agreed to the deal. The next morning was a miracle. He was up and ready before I could even make my coffee. He woke up a few moments before his alarm got in the shower immediately and come down for breakfast completely ready. I was in shock.

Give your child rewards for a good job done.

CHAPTER 20

Hygiene

Confidence is gained when you look, feel, and smell good. As adults we spend so much time on properly caring for our appearance and the way we present ourselves to the world. Please help your child in doing the same. We must care for them and present them to the world with pride and confidence in their appearance. Spend time on them, get their hair cut/properly groom them. Do not send your little girl to school with hair in her face. Do not send your boy to school with a messy mouth and bed head. We need to take pride in our children and show them we care by grooming them properly. Cleaning them and teaching them how to properly clean themselves. I'm sure you can remember the kid who always smelled bad and was a mess to look at. Total confidence killer. We are building confidence and it starts with our appearance.

Make a list of things you must do for each child. Make the time to do their hair and get their hair cut when needed. Build their confidence by making sure their clothes are clean, teeth are brushed, nails are clipped, ears are clean, etc. making them feel good is your job. As a Mom I know the job title has a lengthy list of responsibilities, but this is by far one that tops the charts.

Hygiene:
Teeth brush – morning and night
Hair brush – Everyday - Cut - boys 1x a month girl 1x every 3 months
Nails clipped – 2x a month
Ears q-tipped- everyday
Bathed everyday – Wash hair and body (playtime)
Clean clothes – Pj, underwear, socks, pants, shirt, dresses
Clean sheets
Clean room
Vacuumed room.
Animal mess cleaned up
Chapstick- everyday
(kids lips tend to dry out on a regular basis do not let them go with chapped lips it hurts)

Bandage their wounds – Do not let them scar out. Scabs will be picked – keep them moist and protected

As they get older it is harder to care for them but please

be persistent. Teenagers need extra guidance with this. If your 14-15-year-old still has not developed good habits in brushing their teeth than you still need to do it for them. Do not let your child go smelling bad or without their hair done or teeth brushed. This is a necessity towards their future. You want them to be able to know how to care for themselves and their surroundings. This can also be a chance for you to brush up on your own hygiene. Take care of the dishes and the house. You and your surroundings are all a part of good hygiene.

My rule is if I have not used it in the last 2 years then it needs to go. My parents, as we were growing up always kept a bag of old tooth brushes below the sink. I understand that they are good for cleaning and other stuff but when we got to about 10-15 it was to much. Just toss out what you don't need. Donate it to others. Sell it on the internet. Facebook has a garage sale tab. I have purchased so many things from there and sold many things as well. The moment I do not have a need for it anymore it should be gone. Live with only the necessities and you will have room to grow. If you fill your life with worthless out dated junk, then you will perish. That being said, there is a difference between junk and keepsakes. If you can look back 10 years from now and hold this item with reverence, please keep it. My Dad still has all of his vinyl records. He has a grand collection of keepsakes, as some hold great value.

Do some house cleaning and some self-evaluation to reestablish a good home environment? Keep your surroundings clean and you will feel better about yourself. Which brings me to the bathroom. This is the dirtiest place in the house, but it doesn't have to be. Be sure and properly care for the area we are to clean ourselves. Bathroom is to be scrubbed 2-3 x a month if not more. Tub bleached and cared for, toilet wiped down and scrubbed at least 1 a week. Floors swept and mopped, and sink wiped down every 3 days. Take pride in your area of which you are to take care of yourself. Growing up I was always embarrassed of our house. We had animals and it was never clean. As I grew up, I did everything I could to help with the process, so I was able to hold that pride of clean surroundings. Be aware of it and do everything in your power to clean it up.

This also includes your vehicle. If you once had a nice car and now it is lined with French fries and crushed chips, smells a bit like spoiled milk. Take the time, money and energy to go get it cleaned. I love the way my clean car feels and smells. I even went a step further and I steam cleaned the back seat because something was spilled. Kids are messy and if you spend any amount of time in the car then it's guaranteed your car is a disaster. It doesn't take much for a nice vehicle to go to trash. A few weeks and a few kids are all it takes. Vomit is all over the back seat and if you don't take action then your brand-new car is scared with vomit smell for eternity. No good. So, take the extra step into cleaning the car once a week or so and have that good clean feeling every time you step into the car. It will alleviate the stress of being soccer Mom, taxi and chauffeur. So, we have personal hygiene and surrounding hygiene. What about emotional hygiene/spiritual hygiene? When was the last time you cleared your head space or had a moment to yourself to check in and see what is going on with you internally? There is a lot more under the surface then there is outwardly. You're like an ice burg and if you don't check in with the other half under the surface the titanic (your kids) will come along rub you the wrong way and they will sink. This is a bit more difficult to clean up because we spend so much time worrying about everything else there is no time left for yourself. Especially if you are a working parent. We barely have enough time to cook dinner clean on the weekends and get the kids to school on time there is no way we can spend time on much else.

CHAPTER 21

Release the Mayhem

You must release your emotional baggage in order to find cleanliness within. Keep a journal and write down your successes and your failures for the day. This will set a foundation to grow on. Forgive yourself for your failures and develop a plan to tackle them better in the future. You must remember as your children grow so do you and we are developing life skills in ourselves and them. It must start with you first.

Teach and listen,
Make anything possible,
Never raise your voice,

Never rush,
Never criticize,
Slowdown, Pause,
Take a chill pill,
and spend some quality time with your Family.

You only have a few short years to teach them how to become independent successful adults. Give them the tools to succeed and build life skills on a daily. Equip them properly to handle life on a day to day and become full proficient in living positive lives. Each good choice will lead them on a road to success and set them up to receive blessing of abundance and happiness in the future. Go Now and Serve the Lord and shine his light upon the children of the world.

"Let the little children come, do not
hinder them, for the kingdom of
God belongs to such as these." **– Matthew 19:14**

DEDICATION

I did not start off as a good parent. I was yelling and fighting with my child on a regular basis. I was crying and searching for a answer as to what I was doing wrong. My child would not listen, behave or do anything I wanted him to. I was Lost. Thus, began my Journey to finding an answer. I read countless parenting books and even enrolled in parenting classes. I became a preschool teacher which helped in my journey tremendously. My son as my biggest teacher. He guided me into the person I am today, caring, loving, patient, kind. None of which I would use to describe myself before. He saved my life and I am forever grateful. God found me when he was very young, guided my path and had changed my life forever. I share this book with you as a beginning of a beautiful Journey into the unknown. Thank you for being here with me and know that there is a better version of yourself, waiting to be found. Always choose patience and kindness in the midst of chaos. Show these little ones love and compassion to grow their confidence. Watch them turn into woman and men that are bold, honorable, full of integrity and ready to take on life.